OUR EARTH IN ACTION

VOLCANOES

Chris Oxlade

FRANKLIN WATTS
LONDON•SYDNEY

First published in 2009 by Franklin Watts

Franklin Watts
338 Euston Road
London NW1 3BH

Franklin Watts Australia
Level 17/207 Kent Street
Sydney, NSW 2000

A CIP catalogue record for this book is available
from the British Library.

Dewey number: 551.21

ISBN 978 0 7496 9022 9

Printed in China

Franklin Watts is a division of Hachette Children's Books,
an Hachette UK company.
www.hachette.co.uk

Artwork: John Alston
Editor: Sarah Ridley
Design: Thomas Keenes
Editor in Chief: John C. Miles
Art director: Jonathan Hair

Picture credits:
Byolkov Kirill Alexandrovich/Shutterstock: 4. Philippe Bourseiller/Getty Images: 12, 22. Henri
Faure/istockphoto: 10b. Alexander Forteiny/istockphoto: 13. Fotos International/Rex Features: 24, 25.
Gallo/Getty Images: 9t. Alberto Garcia/Corbis: 17. Julien Grondin/Shutterstock: front cover, 1. Alexander
Hafemann/istockphoto: 15b. Craig Hanson/istockphoto: 10t. Amy Nicole Harris/Shutterstock: 9b. Annette
Soumillard Hemis/Corbis: 20b. Elena Korenbaum/istockphoto: 29c. NASA: 16, 23. Christopher Pillitz/Getty
Images: 19b. Joseph Pollard/istockphoto: 15t. Roger Ressmeyer/Corbis: 14, 21. Sipa Press/Rex Features: 5,
18, 19t, 26, 27. Paul Souders/Getty Images: 7cr. Roger-Viollet/Rex Features: 28. Every attempt has been
made to clear copyright. Should there be any inadvertent omission please apply to the publisher for rectification.

CONTENTS

ABOUT VOLCANOES

What do you think of when you hear the word volcano? A cone-shaped mountain with lava coming from the top? In reality a volcano is simply a place where hot, molten rock from deep underground comes to the surface. Some volcanoes are cone-shaped, others have low, sloping sides. All volcanic eruptions change the landscape, while some cause destruction and death, and can even alter the world's climates.

VOLCANIC ERUPTIONS

When material comes from a volcano, we say that the volcano is erupting. The molten rock that rises into a volcano is called magma. As it erupts from a volcano, magma produces lava, ash and gases. Lava is often blasted into the air by escaping gases and forms lava flows that move down the volcano's slopes. Ash forms towering clouds in the atmosphere and deadly hot avalanches and settles in deep layers on the ground. It can also mix with water to create destructive mud flows.

▲ *Lava blasts from the crater of a volcano, forming a lava fountain.*

ERUPTION EFFECTS

Volcanoes build up the landscape by depositing layers of lava and ash. They create entire mountain ranges and islands in the sea. But they also sometimes destroy themselves during eruptions. After an eruption, the land around a volcano can be smothered by solidified lava flows or a blanket of ash. Lava flows, pyroclastic flows and mud flows can reach areas tens of kilometres from a volcano, and they destroy everything they hit – including buildings. Millions of people live close to volcanoes. Volcanologists attempt to understand volcanoes and predict eruptions, in order to save lives.

▼ *These buildings have been destroyed by ash fall and pyroclastic flows.*

Active, dormant and extinct

All volcanoes are classified as active, dormant or extinct. An active volcano is a volcano that is currently erupting or is showing signs of life. A dormant volcano is a volcano that is not erupting, but that is likely to erupt again at some time. An extinct volcano is a volcano that is unlikely ever to erupt again.

EARTH'S STRUCTURE

Volcanic eruptions happen because of the internal structure of the Earth. Extremely high temperatures and rock movements inside the Earth cause magma to be formed.

The magma makes its way to the surface through cracks and other weaknesses in the Earth's crust (its outer layer). Pressure from gases pushes the magma up and out.

THE EARTH'S INSIDES

The Earth has four main layers, each with different properties. At the centre are the inner core and outer core, which are made mostly from iron. Next comes the mantle, made from rocky material. The Earth's outer layer is the crust. It is very thin compared to the other layers — less than 100 km thick everywhere and as little as 6 km thick under the oceans. The crust, together with the very top layer of the mantle, forms a layer called the lithosphere.

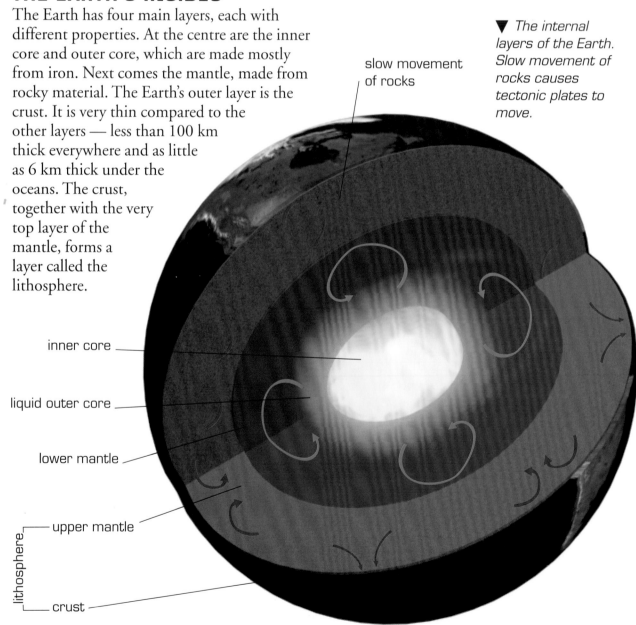

slow movement of rocks

▼ The internal layers of the Earth. Slow movement of rocks causes tectonic plates to move.

inner core

liquid outer core

lower mantle

upper mantle

lithosphere

crust

A CRACKED CRUST

The Earth's lithosphere is cracked into giant pieces (about a dozen in all). These pieces are called tectonic plates. They move around the Earth's surface, but at speeds of only a few centimetres a year. They slide on a layer of weaker rocks in the top layer of the mantle. The movement of the Earth's continents on their tectonic plates is known as continental drift. The lines formed where plates meet each other are called plate boundaries. There are three types of these boundaries. At constructive boundaries the two plates move apart. New rock fills the gap left. At a destructive boundary, two plates move towards each other. Here, the rocks in the plates are crushed together or destroyed. At a conservative boundary, the two plates slide past each other in opposite directions.

▼ This map shows that the location of volcanoes is closely related to tectonic plate boundaries, shown as red dotted lines. Volcano locations are shown as red triangles.

Magma

Magma is the name for molten rock deep underground. Although magma is very hot, the immense pressure deep down stops it from completely melting, so it is very viscous. Many people think that the Earth is full of runny, molten rock, but this is not the case. Instead, there are pockets of magma below the crust. There are also different types of magma, which contain different amounts of different minerals. Magma also contains dissolved gases which play an important role in eruptions.

▼ *Magma turns into lava and gases at the Earth's surface.*

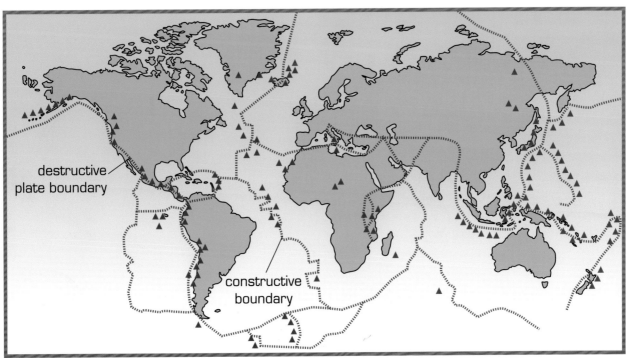

destructive plate boundary

constructive boundary

7

WHERE VOLCANOES HAPPEN

Volcanoes happen along constructive boundaries and destructive boundaries between the Earth's tectonic plates. This is why we see lines of volcanoes around the planet.

The movement of the tectonic plates causes magma to be produced, and the magma tries to rise to the surface. Volcanoes also form over places called hot spots.

VOLCANOES AT CONSTRUCTIVE BOUNDARIES

Two plates move very slowly apart at a constructive plate boundary. Rock from the mantle rises and cools, and forms new crust between the plates. Some of the rock melts as it rises because the pressure on it is reduced, forming magma that rises to the surface, where it creates volcanoes. Most constructive plate boundaries are under the oceans, so most of these volcanoes are hidden under water.

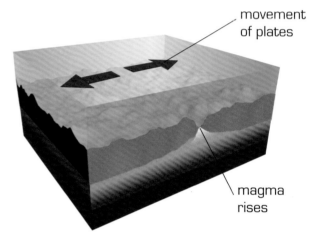

▲ Two tectonic plates move apart at a constructive plate boundary.

VOLCANOES AT DESTRUCTIVE BOUNDARIES

Normally, one plate slides under another at a destructive plate boundary. This process is called subduction, and the area around the boundary is called a subduction zone. Heat from the mantle makes some of the rock in the sinking plate melt, producing magma. Seawater trapped in the plate also helps to produce magma. The magma pushes its way up through the plate above, and if it reaches the surface, forms volcanoes. Volcanoes form in a line parallel to the plate boundary. They can form chains of islands or mountain ranges along the edges of continents, such as the Andes. The Ring of Fire is the name given to a line of volcanoes along the destructive boundaries that surround the giant tectonic plate under the Pacific Ocean.

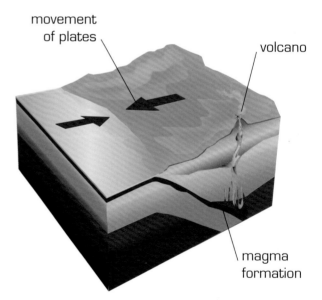

▲ Two tectonic plates move towards each other at a destructive plate boundary.

▼ *Volcanoes at a destructive plate boundary.*

Hot spots

In a few places around the world, volcanoes form in the middle of plates, far away from plate boundaries. These places are known as hot spots. Scientists think that magma pushes up into the crust in these places, forming mantle plumes. The most famous hot spot volcanoes are the ones on the Hawaiian islands in the Pacific. This chain of islands is formed by the tops of giant seamounts. It has grown over millions of years as the Pacific tectonic plate has slowly moved over the mantle plume below.

▶ *A lava flow on an Hawaiian volcano.*

COMPOSITE CONE VOLCANOES

All volcanoes are made up of layers of material that have erupted from them — solidified lava, loose ash and chunks of rock. But volcanoes come in several different shapes and sizes. Composite cone volcanoes are steep-sided volcanoes made up of layers of ash and lava. Volcanoes with a perfect cone shape are always composite cone volcanoes. This type of volcano normally forms over destructive plate boundaries. They are also known as stratovolcanoes.

▲ This perfectly shaped, snow-capped, composite cone volcano is Mount Fuji in Japan.

▼ An explosive eruption from a composite cone volcano. The magma is blasted into fragments of ash.

EXPLOSIVE ERUPTIONS

Composite cone volcanoes tend to erupt violently. The magma that feeds them is very viscous. As it rises, the dissolved gases in it form bubbles, but these can't easily escape through the magma. Instead the gases build up immense pressure and then blast out of the vent at huge speeds. They rip the magma into tiny fragments which cool quickly in the air, forming ash. Gas, hot air and ash rise upwards, forming clouds called eruption columns. Sometimes there are a series of gigantic explosions (see page 26).

Plinian eruptions

The explosive eruptions from composite cone volcanoes are also known as Plinian eruptions. The word 'Plinian' comes from an ancient Roman writer called Pliny the Younger, who described the ash clouds formed by the eruption of Mount Vesuvius in 79CE. This eruption buried the Roman cities of Pompeii and Herculaneum.

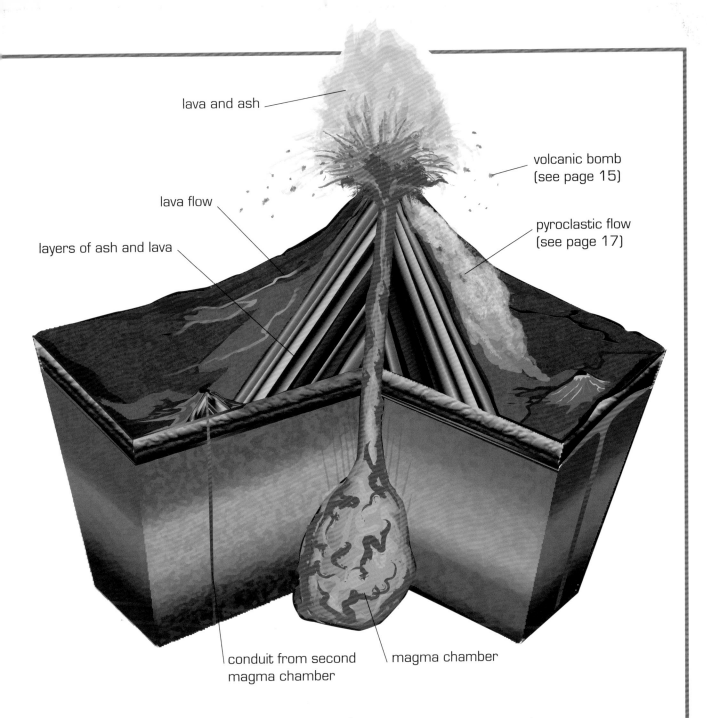

lava and ash

volcanic bomb
(see page 15)

lava flow

pyroclastic flow
(see page 17)

layers of ash and lava

conduit from second
magma chamber

magma chamber

PARTS OF A VOLCANO

Several kilometres under a volcano is a magma chamber – a huge cavern full of magma that feeds the volcano. There is sometimes more than one magma chamber under a volcano. Leading up from the magma chamber is a passageway called a conduit, which carries magma to the surface. The hole at the top of the conduit is called a vent. There are often smaller conduits branching off the main one, leading to side vents. Around the vent is a crater, formed because material is thrown out and up by eruptions. Some volcanoes have two or more craters around their summits, which have been formed by eruptions through different vents.

▲ *The structure of a composite cone volcano. In reality, the magma chamber would be much deeper underground.*

11

SHIELD VOLCANOES AND CINDER CONES

Shield volcanoes are formed by successive layers of lava that flow down their sides. They get their name from their shape as it resembles an upturned warrior's shield (shaped like a shallow bowl). They are low volcanoes, with gently sloping sides. They form over constructive boundaries and hot spots. Cinder cones are volcanoes made up of small chunks of rock. They often form at the side vents of larger volcanoes.

GENTLE ERUPTIONS

The eruptions that form shield volcanoes are gentle compared to the violent eruptions that form composite cone volcanoes. They produce mainly lava and only a little ash. The lava flows down the volcano's slopes and solidifies. Gentle eruptions of lava are known as Hawaiian eruptions because the volcanoes on the Hawaiian islands erupt this way. The eruptions are gentle because the magma from constructive boundaries is quite runny, and it allows gases to escape easily unlike the magma that rises into composite volcanoes, which traps gases because it is quite viscous.

◀ *Lava from a shield volcano flowing into the sea, where it will cool and solidify.*

CINDER CONES

A cinder cone is made up of small chunks of gas-filled rock, called cinders. The chunks are formed when frothy lava solidifies in the air before landing. The chunks gradually build up a cone around the vent. Cinders are also known as scoria, so cinder cones are also known as scoria cones. Similar volcanoes form where a vent is under shallow water. The water makes the eruption more explosive, so ash is formed instead of cinders. The ash falls around the vent and builds up features called tuff rings and tuff cones (tuff is a type of rock formed from layers of ash stuck together).

Measuring explosivity

Volcanologists measure the size of volcanic eruptions on a scale called the Volcanic Explosivity Index (VEI). The more explosive an eruption is, the higher it scores on the scale. The score depends on the amount of lava and ash ejected from the volcano and the height of any eruption column. A very gentle eruption from a shield volcano would score 0 on the scale, but an explosive eruption from a composite cone would score 3 or more.

▼ These are cinder cones on the summit of Mauna Kea, one of the volcanoes on the Hawaiian islands.

LAVA

Lava is molten rock that flows from a volcano's vent. It is formed from the rocky parts of magma, after the magma has released its gases. The lava that erupts from composite cone volcanoes tends to be very viscous. It does not flow well and piles up into heaps called lava domes as it cools. The lava from shield volcanoes tends to be more runny, and forms lava flows. When lava cools, it solidifies and forms solid rock.

LAVA FLOWS

A lava flow is like a river of lava that flows down the sides of a volcano. The speed of a flow depends on the viscosity of the lava and the steepness of the slope. Viscous lava may move just a few metres a day, whilst very runny lava can cover tens of metres per second. There are two different types of solidified lava, known as pahoehoe and aa. Pahoehoe has a smooth, glassy surface, and sometimes looks like coils of rocky rope.

▼ This lava flow is made of solid lava called aa, which is broken into sharp chunks.

Pillow lava

When lava is erupted from vents under the sea, or lava flows from the land into the sea, the surface of the lava cools very quickly. The lava forms into rounded humps that fold over each other. The lumps look a little like pillows, and so this solidified lava is known as pillow lava. Most pillow lava forms over constructive plate boundaries deep under the oceans.

It forms when slow-flowing runny lava solidifies. Aa is made up of sharp chunks of rock, formed when fast-flowing lava solidifies. 'Pahoehoe' and 'aa' are Hawaiian words.

PYROCLASTS

Any volcanic material thrown into the air by gases leaving a vent is called pyroclastic material. Each particle of material is called a pyroclast. The word pyroclast comes from the Greek words for 'fire' and 'broken'. Ash is pyroclastic, so is pumice (which consists of small pieces of lightweight, gas-filled rock), and so are cinders. These all solidify before they hit the ground. Large lumps of lava thrown into the air are called volcanic bombs. Their surfaces cool as they fly through the air, forming a crust. Some bombs land with a splat and some break open like giant eggs.

▲ *This solidified lava is pahoehoe lava. Molten lava is still flowing under the thin crust.*

▼ *Pumice is formed when lumps of frothy lava solidify in the air. It is so light that it floats on water.*

VOLCANIC ASH

Volcanic ash is formed when magma is blasted into fragments during explosive eruptions. The pieces cool quickly, forming solid pieces the size of grains of sand or smaller. Under a microscope, ash particles look like tiny shards of glass. Ash forms huge clouds, avalanches and layers of ash, when it settles on the ground around a volcano.

ASH CLOUDS

Ash is formed during most volcanic eruptions, even gentle ones. However, during the explosive eruptions of composite cone volcanoes, almost all the rising magma is turned to ash. The ash is blasted thousands of metres into the air by high-speed escaping gases. The hot gas and ash heats the surrounding air, and the mixture of gas, air and ash floats still higher into the atmosphere, forming a tall column of ash-filled air called an eruption column or ash cloud. Eruption columns can grow to heights of over 50 km if an eruption continues for days or weeks.

▲ An eruption column rising from a composite cone volcano. Wind is blowing the column to one side.

ASH EFFECTS

Eruption columns spread outwards as they rise, creating a blanket of ash that blocks out the sunlight, turning day to night. The ash can be blown sideways by winds, forming an ash plume that stretches hundreds or even thousands of kilometres from the volcano. The ash gradually settles to the ground, forming deposits called air fall or tephra. On a volcano's slopes these deposits can be many metres deep. The smallest particles of ash are carried furthest, and thin deposits of ash can be left under ash plumes far from a volcano.

PYROCLASTIC FLOWS

Sometimes the ash in the lower part of an ash cloud is so dense that the cloud cannot support itself. It collapses and hurtles down the volcano's slopes. This ash and air avalanche is called a pyroclastic flow. It can also contain lumps of pumice. Inside, the air is filled with dense swirling ash and rock, and the temperature is as high as 600°C. Pyroclastic flows roll forwards at speeds up to 160 kph. Collapsing lava domes also produce pyroclastic flows.

▲ A pyroclastic flow during the eruption of Mount Pinatubo in the Philippines in 1991.

VOLCANO HAZARDS

Compared to other natural disasters, such as earthquakes and famines, volcanic eruptions don't kill that many people. But they are still deadly for people who are in the wrong place at the wrong time. Their unpredictable nature adds to their danger and even experienced volcanologists get caught out. Eruptions also destroy property, infrastructure, crops and livestock when lava, ash and mud flows pour down onto settlements.

LAVA FLOWS

Most lava flows advance downhill fairly slowly, so there is normally plenty of warning that a lava flow is approaching. This means that lava flows are rarely a danger to people. However, lava flows have killed people. In 1977, up to 300 people died when a lava lake at the Nyaragongo volcano in Africa drained suddenly, creating fast lava flows. Lava is molten rock, so it is extremely dense. It knocks things down or carries them along, and its intense heat incinerates anything flammable. Anything that does survive is trapped when the lava solidifies.

ASH

Each particle of volcanic ash is a tiny piece of rock, and a layer of ash even a few centimetres thick is very heavy. Ash often causes roofs to collapse, and is difficult to clear from roads. It is even heavier when soaked by rain. Tiny ash particles find their way into machines, damaging any moving parts because they are so hard and sharp. Wet ash short circuits electrical machinery. Ash also damages and kills crops.

▼ Ash smothers the ground, trees and buildings during the eruption of Mount Pinatubo in the Philippines in 1991.

Volcanic mud flows

When volcanic ash mixes with flowing water it forms mud flows (also called lahars). The water comes from ice and snow that melts because of the heat from the ash landing on it. Also heavy rainfall mixes with ash deposits to create mud flows. The mud is very dense, like wet concrete, and very destructive. In 1985, volcanic mud flows hit the Colombian town of Armero, killing most of the 28,000 inhabitants.

▶ *Workers rescue a child from a volcanic mud flow in Armero.*

PYROCLASTIC FLOWS

The intense heat and high speed of pyroclastic flows means there is no escape for anybody caught by one. Pyroclastic flows have claimed many lives. A pyroclastic flow pulverises and burns anything in its path, and buries the remains in ash. People or animals caught in the flow die when their lungs breathe in the hot gases.

▼ *Buildings buried by volcanic ash on the Caribbean island of Montserrat.*

LIVING WITH VOLCANOES

Millions of people live around volcanoes, where they are in reach of lava flows, pyroclastic flows, mud flows and falls of heavy ash. They live in these hazard zones for many reasons. The soil around volcanoes is rich in nutrients, so is excellent for farming, and many towns and cities have developed since the last eruptions of nearby volcanoes, and so people are unaware of the dangers. Volcanoes also bring tourism.

ERUPTION PLANS

People around volcanoes are protected by monitoring and planning. Volcanoes close to major centres of population are constantly monitored by scientists. If there are any signs of activity, monitoring is stepped up, so that the scientists can try to predict when an eruption is likely. Careful monitoring is most important at composite cone volcanoes, which have the capacity to cause widespread damage. The authorities of districts around volcanoes have emergency plans in place so that officials and emergency services know how to respond in case of an eruption. They work with scientists to decide if, and when, to order evacuations. Hazard maps drawn up by experts show which areas are most at risk from lava flows, pyroclastic flows and mud flows.

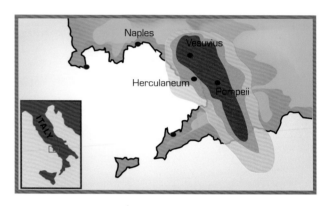

▲ A hazard map for Vesuvius, a volcano near Naples in Italy, which famously erupted in 79CE.

Volcano advantages

There are some advantages to living in volcanic areas of the world. Apart from the rich farming land, there is geothermal energy. This is heat energy taken from the hot rocks underground and used for heating and for electricity generation. Volcanoes and other volcanic features, such as hot springs and geysers, are often a tourist attraction and so bring jobs and money to the local area.

▶ Swimming in the Blue Lagoon, Iceland.

FIGHTING HAZARDS

Volcanic eruptions are driven by enormous forces within the Earth. It is impossible for us to stop them from happening. However, we can try to reduce the destruction they bring to property. In Japan and Indonesia cities are protected from mud flows by special dams designed to trap the mud. People have also tried to divert lava flows away from villages and towns by building embankments, digging ditches and even by bombing. In 1973, at the Icelandic town of Heimaey, a major lava flow was stopped by pouring seawater onto it for many weeks.

▲ *Japanese school children wear hard hats in case of pyroclasts from the nearby erupting volcano.*

VOLCANO SCIENCE

Scientists who study volcanoes are called volcanologists. They try to understand what makes volcanoes erupt, how different sorts of magma behave, what happens inside volcanoes and how lava flows advance, ash clouds grow and pyroclastic flows move. Most importantly they monitor active volcanoes and try to predict when they might erupt. Specialist equipment helps them to monitor dormant volcanoes and study eruptions when they occur.

EQUIPMENT AND TECHNIQUES

Volcanologists make use of a wide range of specialist equipment to monitor volcanoes. One of their most useful tools is an instrument called a seismometer. This measures vibrations in the ground and so is used to detect earthquakes. Eruptions normally begin with earthquakes from under the volcano, caused by magma moving upwards.

▼ *Volcanologists in heat-resistant suits measure the temperature of lava.*

The earthquakes become stronger and more frequent as the eruption progresses. Tiltmeters measure the slope of the ground. They are placed on the slopes of a volcano and detect if the ground swells upwards, which indicates magma pressure building inside the volcano. Volcanologists also use surveying equipment such as laser distance measuring machines and GPS receivers to detect ground movements. Networks of instruments linked to computers allow scientists to build up a three-dimensional picture of what is happening. Volcanologists also monitor any gases coming from a volcano's vents, as the eruption of gases shows that magma is rising towards the surface.

Building hazard maps

Volcanic hazard maps show the areas around a volcano which are at risk from lava flows, ash air fall, pyroclastic flows and mud flows. They indicate high-risk, medium-risk and low-risk areas. These maps are vital for emergency planning. Scientists build hazard maps by studying reports of previous eruptions and surveying old lava and ash deposits.

REMOTE SENSING

Remote sensing (using information from satellites) is another useful tool for monitoring volcanoes. Heat-detecting cameras show the temperature of the ground, which can indicate that an eruption is imminent. Radar measurements build up a three-dimensional picture of a volcano's shape. Finally, satellite photographs show the spread of ash plumes from a volcano.

▼ *An infra-red satellite image of Mount Etna, a volcano in Sicily.*

CASE STUDY: MOUNT ST HELENS

Mount St Helens is one of a series of volcanoes in the Cascade Range of mountains in North America. These volcanoes have grown over a subduction zone along North America's west coast. Mount St Helens is famous for an eruption of staggering violence in 1980. The eruption blew the top off the mountain, devastated the countryside around and killed 57 people, including volcanologists.

FIRST SIGNS

Old ash deposits show that Mount St Helens has been active for at least 40,000 years. In 1980 it had been dormant for more than a century. In March that year instruments detected clusters of small earthquakes, which were soon followed by eruptions of steam and gas. During April a bulge grew on the north flank of the volcano. By the middle of May it was 80 m high. It was obvious that an eruption was imminent.

▶ A giant eruption column grew from Mount St Helens in the hours after the initial lateral blast.

THE RESPONSE

Volcanologists monitored the situation and advised the authorities. The mountain itself was closed to climbers in March. As the bulge grew, an exclusion zone was set up, which was gradually widened as the weeks passed. The promise of a major eruption brought sightseers and media organisations to the area, and many ignored the exclusions. Eventually America's National Guard had to be brought in to keep people away.

▼ The lateral blast from Mount St Helens felled millions of trees around the volcano.

THE ERUPTION

On 18 May the bulge collapsed in a giant avalanche. The pressure on the magma below was instantly released, and the gases in it expanded explosively. Hot ash and rock were blasted sideways (an event known as a lateral blast). An eruption column was also thrown upwards. The lateral blast acted like a super-powerful pyroclastic flow. It raced 30 km over hills and across valleys, stripping the countryside bare.

St Helens' victims

The power of the eruption at Mount St Helens was greater than any experts had expected. The lateral blast also came as a surprise. It meant that areas outside the exclusion zone north of the mountain were affected. This is where most victims died. They included campers, tourists, forestry workers and even volcanologists, who thought they were out of harm's way.

CASE STUDY: PINATUBO

Pinatubo is a composite cone volcano in the Philippines, about 50 km from the major city of Manila. Its eruption in 1991 was the most explosive eruption of the 20th century. The eruption came as a surprise, as Pinatubo had been dormant for 600 years.

FIRST SIGNS AND RESPONSE

In early April 1991 eruptions of steam were seen coming from the summit of the forest-covered mountain. Locals reported these to the authorities. Scientists from the Philippines and the USA set up an observatory at the nearby Clark Air Base and began to monitor the volcano's activity. They detected swarms of earthquakes. The scientists surveyed the area around the volcano and drew up hazard maps for pyroclastic flows and mud flows. In May and June more gas eruptions forced the authorities to set up an exclusion zone, which was gradually widened. By the middle of June the exclusion zone stretched 30 km from the volcano, and nearly 60,000 people had been evacuated.

▲ Ash blasted from the summit crater of Mount Pinatubo at hundreds of kilometres per hour.

THE ERUPTION

Pinatubo's main eruption began on 15 June and had a VEI of 6 (see page 13). There were several giant explosions in the following days, which threw up an eruption column 40 km high. Pyroclastic flows travelled up to 20 km from the summit, leaving the landscape buried in ash. The eruption continued for weeks, and stopped in September.

PINATUBO'S DAMAGE

The exclusion zones and evacuations around Pinatubo were a result of excellent monitoring and emergency planning. They almost certainly saved thousands of lives. However, there were about 900 deaths. Some people died as their houses collapsed under the weight of ash. Others died in mud flows set off by torrential rain caused by the arrival of Typhoon Yunya in the days after the main eruption. In the months and years after the eruption, seasonal rains caused mud flows that smothered a huge area of important agricultural land, and destroyed tens of thousands of homes. Mud flows continue to be a hazard during heavy rains.

▶ Ash fall was a major hazard at Pinatubo. Many houses collapsed under the weight of ash on their roofs.

GIANT ERUPTIONS

The eruptions of Mount St Helens and Pinatubo were incredibly violent events. However, they were relatively minor compared to some eruptions in the distant past. These 'supervolcano' eruptions were so explosive that they affected the whole planet. There is plenty of evidence for these eruptions, including ancient ash deposits and giant depressions called calderas, formed when the ground collapsed into vast, empty magma chambers. Inevitably there will be supervolcano eruptions in the future.

TAMBORA, KRAKATAU, TOBA

In 1815 a composite cone volcano called Tambora in Indonesia erupted. The eruption had a VEI of 7 (see page 13), and was possibly the most violent eruption of the last 10,000 years. Ash and gas blown into the atmosphere caused cold weather in many parts of the world, which in turn caused crops failures and famines. In 1883 the volcanic island of Krakatau suffered a large eruption that destroyed most of the

▼ The Indonesian island of Krakatau, which was destroyed by a giant eruption in 1883.

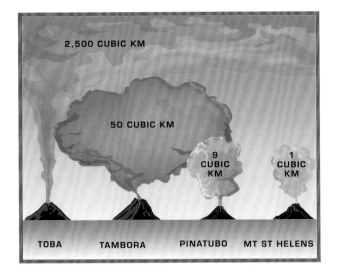

2,500 CUBIC KM

50 CUBIC KM

9 CUBIC KM

1 CUBIC KM

TOBA   TAMBORA   PINATUBO   MT ST HELENS

Global effects

Giant eruptions throw vast amounts of ash and gases (mostly sulphur dioxide) high into the atmosphere. The ash and gas are spread around the globe by high-level winds, where they block sunlight from reaching the ground. This cools the climate. Sulphur dioxide is also released during eruptions of lava. About 65 million years ago, a giant lava eruption in India could have created climate change and contributed to the end of the dinosaurs.

▲ *This chart shows relative amounts of material ejected by some of the volcanic eruptions mentioned in this book.*

volcano's cone (see page 28) and also disrupted world weather patterns. Toba is also in Indonesia. Its eruption, about 74,000 years ago, had a VEI of 8. It produced about fifty times as much ash as Tambora, and left a caldera 100 km across. The event caused a global temperature drop of about 4°C, possibly for several years. Experts think the human race only just survived this catastrophic eruption.

▲ *Crater Lake in Oregon, USA, fills a massive caldera left by a giant eruption about 7,700 years ago.*

FUTURE ERUPTIONS

There will be eruptions of supervolcanoes in the future. One likely place is Yellowstone in the USA. A supervolcano has erupted here several times in the last few million years, and another eruption is due some time soon (but it might not be for tens of thousands of years). The effects that such an event would have on the world's population are unthinkable. But it will almost certainly happen one day. The only question for volcanologists is where, and when.

GLOSSARY

ash cloud *see* eruption column

ash fall ash that falls from an ash cloud and settles to the ground

ash tiny particles of solidified magma

caldera a giant hole formed when the ground collapses into an empty magma chamber after an eruption

cinder cone a small cone-shaped volcano formed by millions of small chunks of solidified frothy lava

climate the long-term pattern of weather that a place experiences

composite cone a steep-sided volcano made up of layers of ash and lava

constructive plate boundary a line along which two tectonic plates are moving apart

crater a dish-shaped hole at the summit of a volcano

crust the rocky top layer of the Earth

destructive plate boundary a line along which the edges of two tectonic plates are moving towards each other

dormant describes a volcano that is not erupting, but is likely to erupt again

eruption column a tall ash-filled cloud formed during a volcanic eruption

gas eruption when gases emerge from a volcano's vent

geyser an intermittent hot-water fountain caused by hot rocks underground boiling water

hazard map a map of an area showing areas that are likely to be hit by lava flows, pyroclastic flows, mud flows or ash fall during a volcanic eruption

hot spot a place far from any tectonic plate boundary where magma forces its way to the surface

hot spring a place where water heated by hot rocks emerges from underground

lava dome a heap of solidified lava usually formed around the vent of a composite cone volcano

lava the name given to the molten, rocky part of magma when it comes out of a volcano

lithosphere the top layer of the Earth's mantle and the crust form the lithosphere. It is cracked into tectonic plates (see below)

magma molten rock underground

mantle the thick layer of rock inside the Earth under the crust

mud flow (lahar) a fast-flowing mixture of volcanic ash and water

plate boundary the line along which two tectonic plates meet

pyroclast any lump of lava or rock thrown into the air during an eruption

pyroclastic flow a cloud made up of extremely hot gas, ash and rock that flows down the side of a volcano like an avalanche

refugee camp a camp set up for people who have been forced to move from their homes for some reason

seamount a volcano that grows up from the ocean floor

shield volcano a volcano with gently sloping sides, made entirely from solidified lava flows

tectonic plate one of the huge pieces that make up the Earth's lithosphere

vent a hole on a volcano where magma emerges from underground

viscous describes a liquid that does not flow easily, like treacle

volcanic bomb a large lump of lava thrown into the air during an eruption

volcanologist a scientist who studies volcanoes

Further information

Global Volcanism Program
Information on active volcanoes around the world.
http://www.volcano.si.edu/

US Geological Survey
Lots of science, news and links on volcanoes.
http://www.usgs.gov/hazards/volcanoes

Also links to hundreds of volcanoes at:
http://vulcan.wr.usgs.gov/Volcanoes/

Mount St Helens
The US Geological Survey site for Mount St Helens, with information about the 1980 eruption and recent activity.
http://vulcan.wr.usgs.gov/Volcanoes/MSH/

Montserrat Volcano Observatory
Information and photographs on this active volcano.
http://www.mvo.ms/

Pyroclastic flows
Amazing video of a pyroclastic flow.
http://faculty.gg.uwyo.edu/heller/SedMovs/Pyroclastic.htm

Volcano World
Contains links to other volcano sites, photos and videos.
http://www.volcanoworld.org

NOTE TO PARENTS AND TEACHERS:
Every effort has been made by the Publishers to ensure that the websites in this book are suitable for children, that they are of the highest educational value, and that they contain no inappropriate or offensive material. However, because of the nature of the Internet, it is impossible to guarantee that the contents of these sites will not be altered. We strongly advise that Internet access is supervised by a responsible adult.

INDEX